My Bilingual Picture Book

Il mio libro illustrato bilingue

Sefa's most beautiful children's stories in one volume

Ulrich Renz • Barbara Brinkmann:

Sleep Tight, Little Wolf · Dormi bene, piccolo lupo

For ages 2 and up

Cornelia Haas • Ulrich Renz:

My Most Beautiful Dream · Il mio più bel sogno

For ages 2 and up

Ulrich Renz • Marc Robitzky:

The Wild Swans · I cigni selvatici

Based on a fairy tale by Hans Christian Andersen

For ages 5 and up

© 2024 by Sefa Verlag Kirsten Bödeker, Lübeck, Germany. www.sefa-verlag.de

Special thanks to Paul Bödeker, Freiburg, Germany

All rights reserved.

ISBN: 9783756304363

Read · Listen · Understand

Sleep Tight, Little Wolf
Dormi bene, piccolo lupo

Ulrich Renz / Barbara Brinkmann

English   bilingual   Italian

Translation:

Pete Savill (English)

Margherita Haase (Italian)

Audiobook and video:

www.sefa-bilingual.com/bonus

Password for free access:

English: **LWEN1423**

Italian: **LWIT1829**

Good night, Tim! We'll continue searching tomorrow.
Now sleep tight!

Buona notte, Tim! Domani continuiamo a cercare.
Adesso però dormi bene!

It is already dark outside.

Fuori è già buio.

What is Tim doing?

Ma cosa fa Tim?

He is leaving for the playground.

What is he looking for there?

Va al parco giochi.

Che cosa sta cercando?

The little wolf!

He can't sleep without it.

Il piccolo lupo.

Senza di lui non riesce a dormire.

Who's this coming?

Ma chi sta arrivando?

Marie! She's looking for her ball.

Marie! Lei sta cercando la sua palla.

And what is Tobi looking for?

E Tobi cosa cerca?

His digger.

La sua ruspa.

And what is Nala looking for?

E cosa cerca Nala?

Her doll.

La sua bambola.

Don't the children have to go to bed?
The cat is rather surprised.

Ma i bambini non devono andare a letto?
Il gatto si meraviglia.

Who's coming now?

E adesso chi sta arrivando?

Tim's mum and dad!

They can't sleep without their Tim.

La mamma e il papà di Tim.

Senza il loro Tim non riescono a dormire.

More of them are coming! Marie's dad.
Tobi's grandpa. And Nala's mum.

Ed ecco che arrivano anche altri!
Il papà di Marie. Il nonno di Tobi. E la mamma di Nala.

Now hurry to bed everyone!

Ma adesso svelti a letto!

Good night, Tim!

Tomorrow we won't have to search any longer.

Buona notte, Tim!

Domani non dobbiamo più cercare.

Sleep tight, little wolf!

Dormi bene, piccolo lupo!

Cornelia Haas • Ulrich Renz

My Most Beautiful Dream
Il mio più bel sogno

Translation:

Sefâ Jesse Konuk Agnew (English)

Clara Galeati (Italian)

Audiobook and video:

www.sefa-bilingual.com/bonus

Password for free access:

English: **BDEN1423**

Italian: **BDIT1829**

My Most Beautiful Dream
Il mio più bel sogno

Cornelia Haas · Ulrich Renz

English — bilingual — Italian

Lulu can't fall asleep. Everyone else is dreaming already – the shark, the elephant, the little mouse, the dragon, the kangaroo, the knight, the monkey, the pilot. And the lion cub. Even the bear has trouble keeping his eyes open ...

Hey bear, will you take me along into your dream?

Lulù non riesce ad addormentarsi. Tutti gli altri stanno già sognando – lo squalo, l'elefante, il topolino, il drago, il canguro, il cavaliere, la scimmia, il pilota. E il leoncino. Anche all'orso stanno crollando gli occhi ...

Ehi orso, mi porti con te nel tuo sogno?

And with that, Lulu finds herself in bear dreamland. The bear catches fish in Lake Tagayumi. And Lulu wonders, who could be living up there in the trees?

When the dream is over, Lulu wants to go on another adventure. Come along, let's visit the shark! What could he be dreaming?

E così Lulù è già nel paese dei sogni degli orsi. L'orso cattura pesci nel lago Tagayumi. E Lulù si chiede chi potrebbe mai vivere là su quegli alberi? Quando il sogno è finito, Lulù vuole provare qualcos'altro. Vieni, andiamo a trovare lo squalo! Che cosa starà sognando?

The shark plays tag with the fish. Finally he's got some friends! Nobody's afraid of his sharp teeth.

When the dream is over, Lulu wants to go on another adventure. Come along, let's visit the elephant! What could he be dreaming?

Lo squalo sta giocando ad acchiapparella con i pesci. Finalmente ha degli amici! Nessuno ha paura dei suoi denti aguzzi.
Quando il sogno è finito, Lulù vuole provare qualcos'altro. Venite, andiamo a trovare l'elefante! Che cosa starà sognando?

The elephant is as light as a feather and can fly! He's about to land on the celestial meadow.

When the dream is over, Lulu wants to go on another adventure. Come along, let's visit the little mouse! What could she be dreaming?

L'elefante è leggero come una piuma e può volare! Sta per atterrare sul prato celeste.
Quando il sogno è finito, Lulù vuole provare qualcos'altro. Venite, andiamo a trovare il topolino! Che cosa starà sognando?

The little mouse watches the fair. She likes the roller coaster best. When the dream is over, Lulu wants to go on another adventure. Come along, let's visit the dragon! What could she be dreaming?

Il topolino sta guardando la fiera. Gli piacciono particolarmente le montagne russe.

Quando il sogno è finito, Lulù vuole provare qualcos'altro. Venite, andiamo a trovare il drago! Che cosa starà sognando?

The dragon is thirsty from spitting fire. She'd like to drink up the whole lemonade lake.

When the dream is over, Lulu wants to go on another adventure. Come along, let's visit the kangaroo! What could she be dreaming?

Il drago, a furia di sputare fuoco, ha sete. Gli piacerebbe bersi l'intero lago di limonata.

Quando il sogno è finito, Lulù vuole provare qualcos'altro. Venite, andiamo a trovare il canguro! Che cosa starà sognando?

The kangaroo jumps around the candy factory and fills her pouch. Even more of the blue sweets! And more lollipops! And chocolate!
When the dream is over, Lulu wants to go on another adventure. Come along, let's visit the knight! What could he be dreaming?

Il canguro sta saltando nella fabbrica di dolciumi e si riempe il marsupio.
Ancora caramelle blu! E ancora lecca-lecca! E cioccolata!
Quando il sogno è finito, Lulù vuole provare qualcos'altro. Venite, andiamo a trovare il cavaliere! Che cosa starà sognando?

The knight is having a cake fight with his dream princess. Oops! The whipped cream cake has gone the wrong way!

When the dream is over, Lulu wants to go on another adventure. Come along, let's visit the monkey! What could he be dreaming?

Il cavaliere sta facendo una battaglia di torte con la principessa dei suoi sogni. Oh! La torta alla panna va nella direzione sbagliata!
Quando il sogno è finito, Lulù vuole provare qualcos'altro. Venite, andiamo a trovare la scimmia! Che cosa starà sognando?

Snow has finally fallen in Monkeyland. The whole barrel of monkeys is beside itself and getting up to monkey business.

When the dream is over, Lulu wants to go on another adventure. Come along, let's visit the pilot! In which dream could he have landed?

Finalmente ha nevicato in Scimmialandia! L'intera combriccola di scimmie non sta più nella pelle e si comportano tutte come in una gabbia di matti. Quando il sogno è finito, Lulù vuole provare qualcos'altro. Venite, andiamo a trovare il pilota! In che sogno potrebbe essere atterrato?

The pilot flies on and on. To the ends of the earth, and even farther, right on up to the stars. No other pilot has ever managed that.
When the dream is over, everybody is very tired and doesn't feel like going on many adventures anymore. But they'd still like to visit the lion cub.
What could she be dreaming?

Il pilota vola e vola ancora. Fino ai confini della terra e ancora più lontano, fino alle stelle. Non ce l'ha fatta nessun altro pilota.
Quando il sogno è finito, sono già tutti molto stanchi e non vogliono più continuare a provare così tanto. Però il leoncino, vogliono ancora andare a trovarlo. Che cosa starà sognando?

The lion cub is homesick and wants to go back to the warm, cozy bed.
And so do the others.

And thus begins ...

Il leoncino ha nostalgia di casa e vuole tornare nel caldo, accogliente letto.
E gli altri pure.

E là inizia ...

... Lulu's
most beautiful dream.

... il più bel sogno
di Lulù.

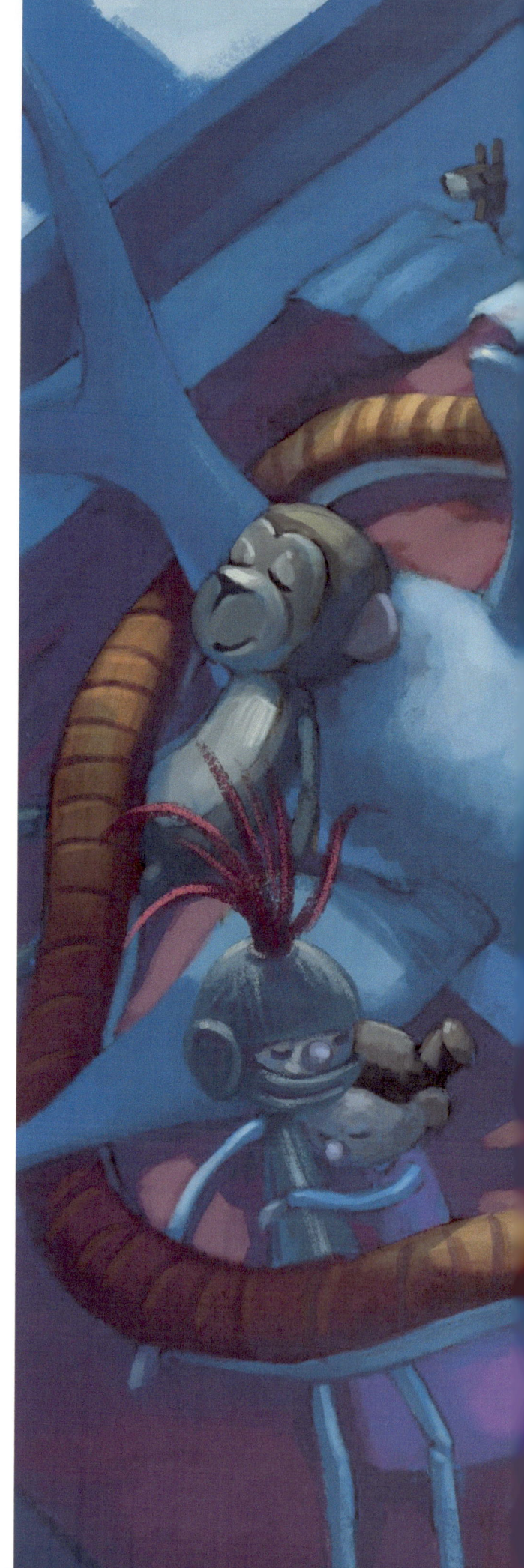

Ulrich Renz • Marc Robitzky

The Wild Swans
I cigni selvatici

Translation:

Ludwig Blohm, Pete Savill (English)

Emanuele Cattani, Clara Galeati (Italian)

Audiobook and video:

www.sefa-bilingual.com/bonus

Password for free access:

```
English: WSEN1423
Italian: WSIT1829
```

Ulrich Renz · Marc Robitzky

The Wild Swans

I cigni selvatici

Based on a fairy tale by

Hans Christian Andersen

English · bilingual · Italian

Once upon a time there were twelve royal children – eleven brothers and one older sister, Elisa. They lived happily in a beautiful castle.

C'erano una volta dodici figli di un re – undici fratelli ed una sorella più grande, Elisa. Vivevano felici in un bellissimo castello.

One day the mother died, and some time later the king married again. The new wife, however, was an evil witch. She turned the eleven princes into swans and sent them far away to a distant land beyond the large forest.

Un giorno la madre morì, e poco tempo dopo il re si risposò. La nuova moglie però era una strega cattiva. Con un incantesimo, trasformò gli undici principi in cigni e li mandò molto lontano, in un Paese al di là della grande foresta.

She dressed the girl in rags and smeared an ointment onto her face that turned her so ugly, that even her own father no longer recognized her and chased her out of the castle. Elisa ran into the dark forest.

Vestì la ragazza di stracci e le spalmò sul volto un orribile unguento, tanto che nemmeno il padre riuscì più a riconoscerla e la cacciò dal castello. Elisa corse nella foresta tenebrosa.

Now she was all alone, and longed for her missing brothers from the depths of her soul. As the evening came, she made herself a bed of moss under the trees.

Ora era completamente sola, e desiderava con tutto il cuore rivedere i suoi fratelli scomparsi. Quando venne la sera, si fece un letto di muschio sotto un albero.

The next morning she came to a calm lake and was shocked when she saw her reflection in it. But once she had washed, she was the most beautiful princess under the sun.

La mattina dopo giunse ad un lago calmo, e rimase sconcertata nel vedere il proprio riflesso nell'acqua. Ma appena si pulì, divenne la più bella principessa sulla faccia della terra.

After many days Elisa reached the great sea. Eleven swan feathers were bobbing on the waves.

Molti giorni dopo, Elisa raggiunse il grande mare. Tra le onde, oscillavano undici piume di cigno.

As the sun set, there was a swooshing noise in the air and eleven wild swans landed on the water. Elisa immediately recognized her enchanted brothers. They spoke swan language and because of this she could not understand them.

Quando il sole tramontò, ci fu un fruscio nell'aria, e undici cigni si posarono sull'acqua. Elisa riconobbe immediatamente i propri fratelli stregati. Ma dato che parlavano la lingua dei cigni, lei non li poté capire.

During the day the swans flew away, and at night the siblings snuggled up together in a cave.

One night Elisa had a strange dream: Her mother told her how she could release her brothers from the spell. She should knit shirts from stinging nettles and throw one over each of the swans. Until then, however, she was not allowed to speak a word, or else her brothers would die.
Elisa set to work immediately. Although her hands were burning as if they were on fire, she carried on knitting tirelessly.

Durante il giorno i cigni volavano via, e la notte si accoccolavano tutti assieme alla sorella in una grotta.

Una notte, Elisa fece uno strano sogno. Sua madre le disse come avrebbe potuto liberare i suoi fratelli. Avrebbe dovuto tessere delle camicie di ortiche per ognuno di loro e poi lanciargliele. Fino a quel momento però, non le era concesso dire una sola parola, altrimenti i suoi fratelli sarebbero morti. Elisa si mise immediatamente al lavoro. Sebbene le mani le bruciassero, continuò a tessere senza stancarsi.

One day hunting horns sounded in the distance. A prince came riding along with his entourage and he soon stood in front of her. As they looked into each other's eyes, they fell in love.

Un giorno, si sentirono corni da caccia in lontananza. Un principe venne cavalcando con il suo seguito e presto le fu di fronte. Non appena i due si guardarono negli occhi, si innamorarono.

The prince lifted Elisa onto his horse and rode to his castle with her.

Il principe fece salire Elisa sul cavallo e la condusse al proprio castello.

The mighty treasurer was anything but pleased with the arrival of the silent beauty. His own daughter was meant to become the prince's bride.

Il potente tesoriere fu tutto fuorché felice dell'arrivo della principessa muta. La propria figlia sarebbe dovuta diventare la sposa del principe.

Elisa had not forgotten her brothers. Every evening she continued working on the shirts. One night she went out to the cemetery to gather fresh nettles. While doing so she was secretly watched by the treasurer.

Elisa non si era dimenticata dei suoi fratelli. Ogni sera continuava il suo lavoro sulle camicie. Una notte uscì per andare al cimitero a cogliere delle ortiche fresche. Il tesoriere la osservò di nascosto.

As soon as the prince was away on a hunting trip, the treasurer had Elisa thrown into the dungeon. He claimed that she was a witch who met with other witches at night.

Non appena il principe partì per una battuta di caccia, il tesoriere gettò Elisa nelle segrete. Affermò che fosse una strega che si incontrava con altre streghe durante la notte.

At dawn, Elisa was fetched by the guards. She was going to be burned to death at the marketplace.

All'alba, Elisa venne presa da delle guardie, per venir poi bruciata nella piazza del mercato.

No sooner had she arrived there, when suddenly eleven white swans came flying towards her. Elisa quickly threw a shirt over each of them. Shortly thereafter all her brothers stood before her in human form. Only the smallest, whose shirt had not been quite finished, still had a wing in place of one arm.

Non appena fu lì, arrivarono undici cigni bianchi volando. Elisa lanciò rapidamente una camicia a ciascuno di loro. Poco dopo, tutti i suoi fratelli si trovarono dinanzi a lei con sembianze umane. Solo il più piccolo, la cui camicia non era stata del tutto completata, mantenne un'ala al posto di un braccio.

The siblings' joyous hugging and kissing hadn't yet finished as the prince returned. At last Elisa could explain everything to him. The prince had the evil treasurer thrown into the dungeon. And after that the wedding was celebrated for seven days.

And they all lived happily ever after.

I fratelli si stavano ancora baciando e abbracciando quando arrivò il principe. Finalmente Elisa gli poté spiegare tutto. Il principe fece rinchiudere il tesoriere malvagio nelle segrete. Dopodiché, si celebrò il matrimonio per sette giorni.

E vissero tutti felici e contenti.

Hans Christian Andersen

Hans Christian Andersen was born in the Danish city of Odense in 1805, and died in 1875 in Copenhagen. He gained world fame with his literary fairy-tales such as „The Little Mermaid", „The Emperor's New Clothes" and „The Ugly Duckling". The tale at hand, „The Wild Swans", was first published in 1838. It has been translated into more than one hundred languages and adapted for a wide range of media including theater, film and musical.

Barbara Brinkmann was born in Munich in 1969 and grew up in the foothills of the Bavarian Alps. She studied architecture in Munich and is currently a research associate in the Department of Architecture at the Technical University of Munich. She also works as a freelance graphic designer, illustrator, and author.

Cornelia Haas has been illustrating childrens' and adolescents' books since 2001. She was born near Augsburg, Germany, in 1972. She studied design at the Münster University of Applied Sciences and is currently a professor on the faculty of Münster University of Applied Sciences teaching illustration.

Marc Robitzky, born in 1973, studied at the Technical School of Art in Hamburg and the Academy of Visual Arts in Frankfurt. He works as a freelance illustrator and communication designer in Aschaffenburg (Germany).

Ulrich Renz was born in Stuttgart, Germany, in 1960. After studying French literature in Paris he graduated from medical school in Lübeck and worked as head of a scientific publishing company. He is now a writer of non-fiction books as well as children's fiction books.

Do you like drawing?

Here are the pictures from the story to color in:

www.sefa-bilingual.com/coloring

www.ingramcontent.com/pod-product-compliance
Lightning Source LLC
LaVergne TN
LVHW070447080526
838202LV00035B/2764